CHICKEN WIN

AIRPL
COLORING BOOK
BLUE SKIES

ISBN 978-1-4951-1671-1

Published by Michael and Stefan Strasser
www.chickenwingscomics.com
info@chickenwingscomics.com

Printed in the USA by The Printing House Inc., Wisconsin.

Thanks to Mrs. Breaux's 4th & 5th graders at Summerville Elementary School for helping with this book.

A Piper J-3 Cub is flying high above the clouds.

Oh no! Chuck caught more than he bargained for!

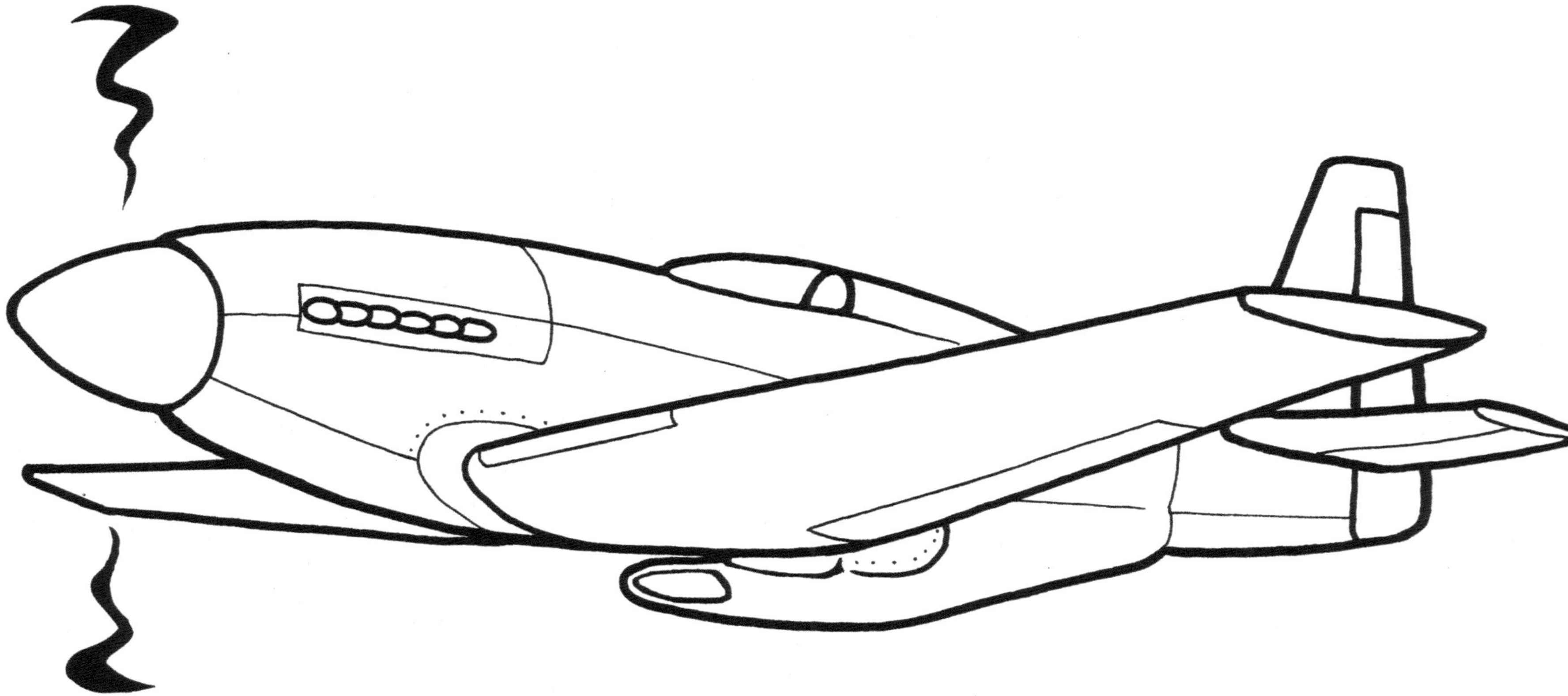

A North American P-51 *Mustang* has been converted into a Racing Airplane.

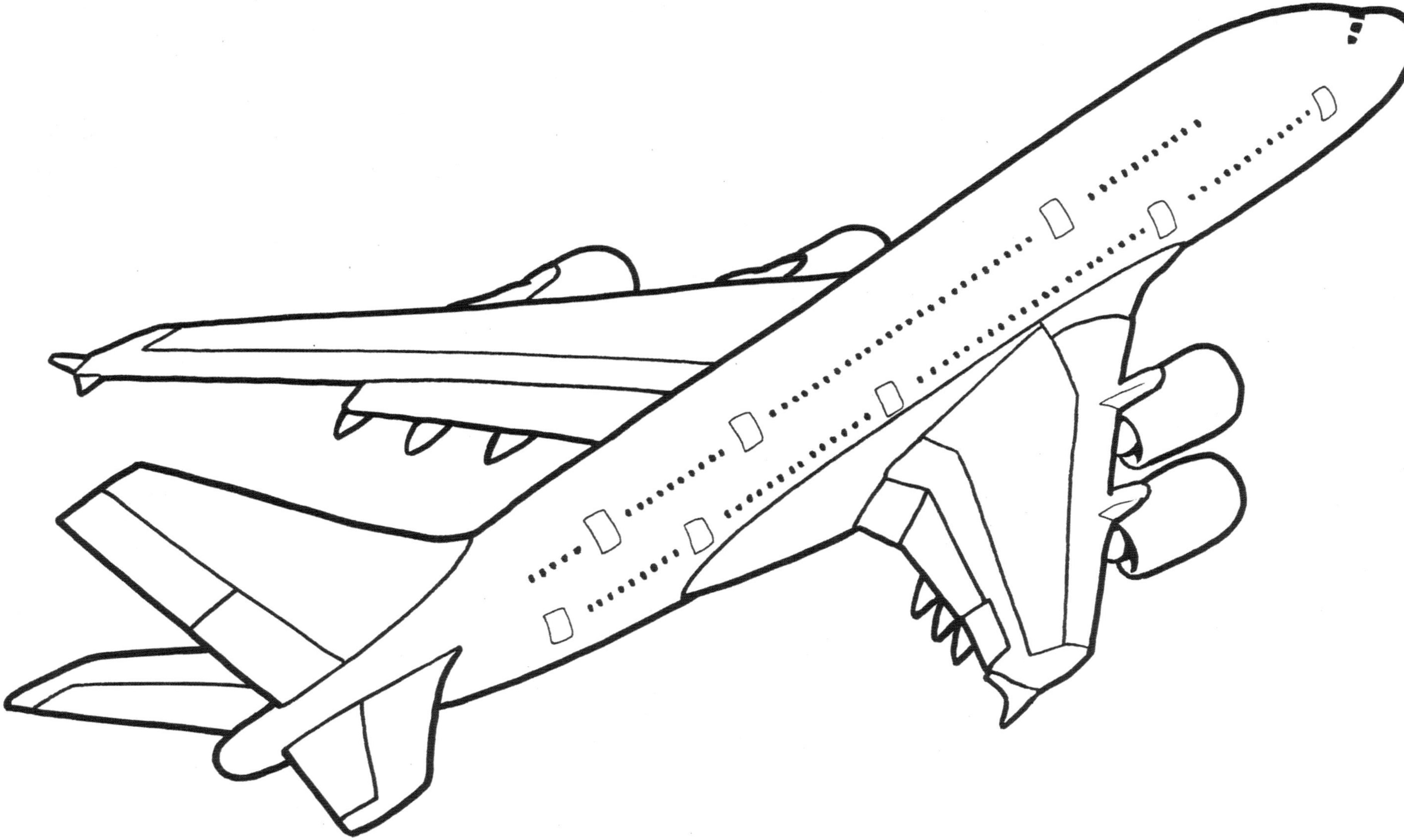

The Airbus A380 is the world's biggest passenger plane.
It is so big that it can carry up to 850 people.

Chuck is flying a Zlin 50 LX.

Chuck is lost in the clouds with his helicopter.
Can you help him find his way out of the clouds?

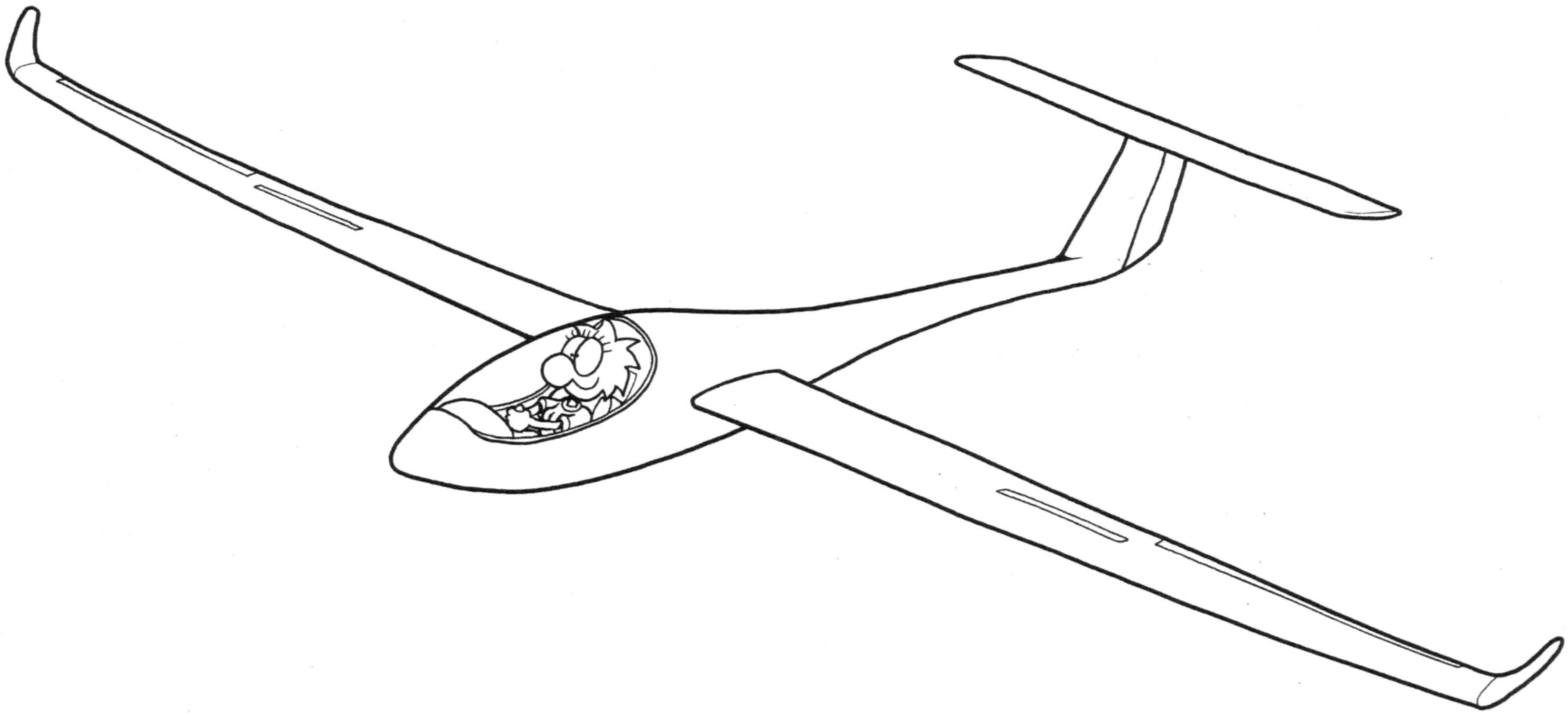

Gliders have no engines or propellers. They fly solely by using the rising air that is heated by the sun.

A Sikorsky S-64 Skycrane picks up water with its snorkel to dump it on the forest fire in the background.

Chuck is flying an Aerocomp Esqual.

A Single Engine Air Tanker is dropping
water on a forest fire.

Connect the dots!

A hot air balloon flies because the hot air in the balloon is lighter than the cold air surrounding it.

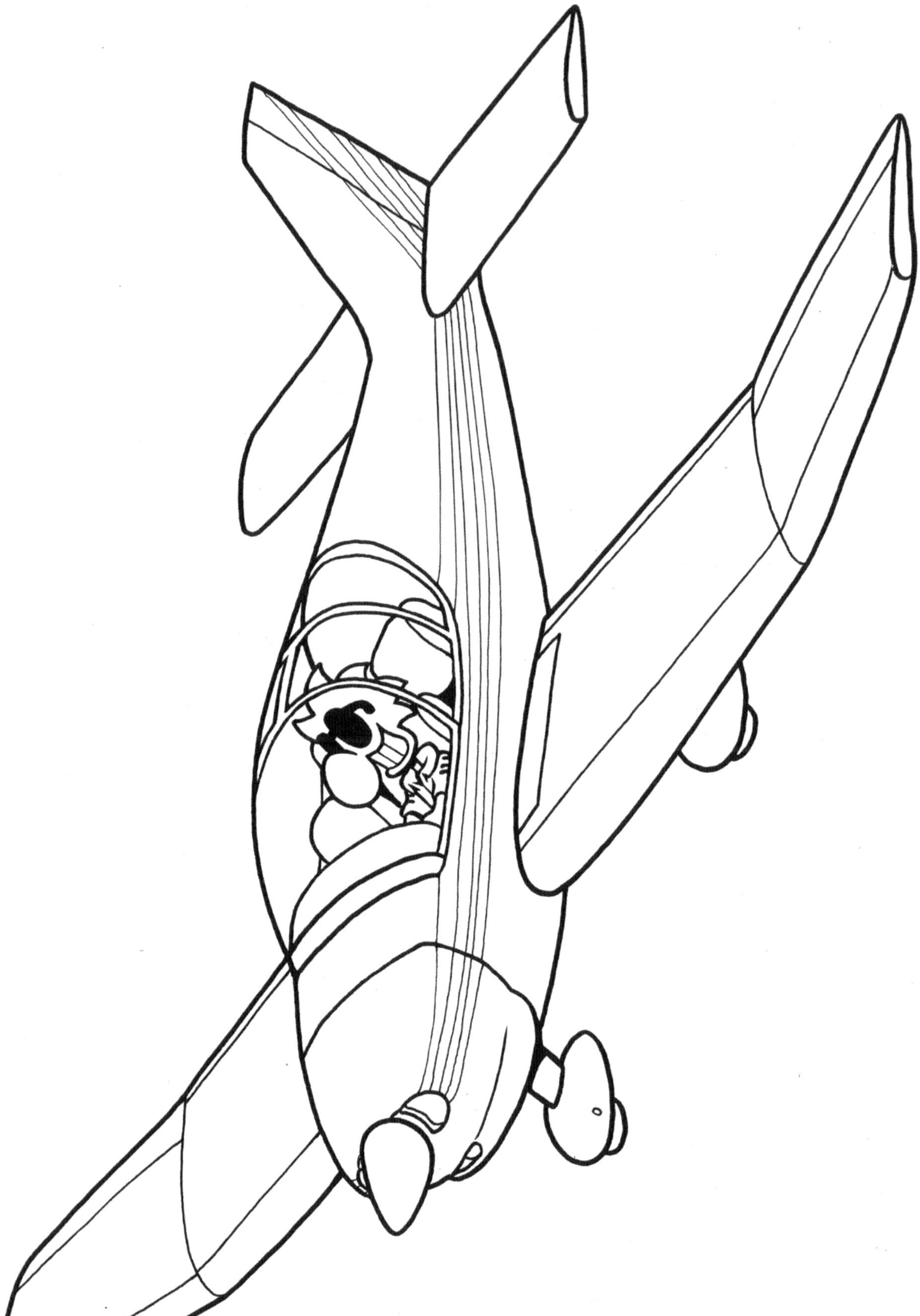

Chuck takes to the air in a French Robin DR 400.

This seaplane has floats instead of wheels,
so it can land on water.

Oh no! Chuck has hurt himself while skiing.
Help the rescue helicopter find its way to him.

A Grumman F-14 Tomcat breaks through the clouds.

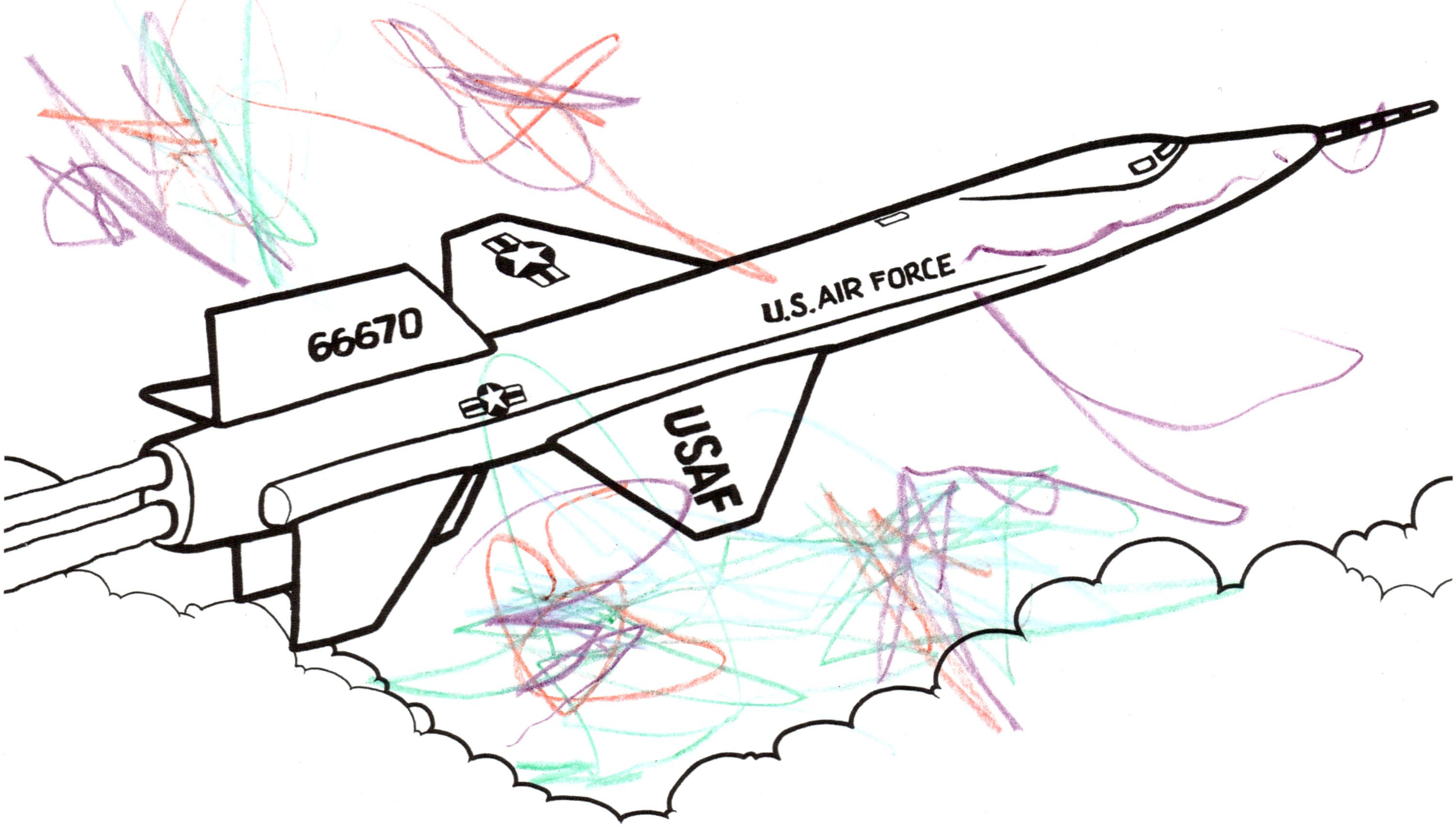

The North American X-15 holds the official world record for the highest speed ever reached by a manned, powered aircraft.

Chuck cruises along in a Diamond DA 40.

The F-117 Nighthawk is a stealth airplane.
It is almost impossible to detect it with radar.

Can you tell which aircraft transports what cargo?
Draw lines to match the aircraft to the cargo.

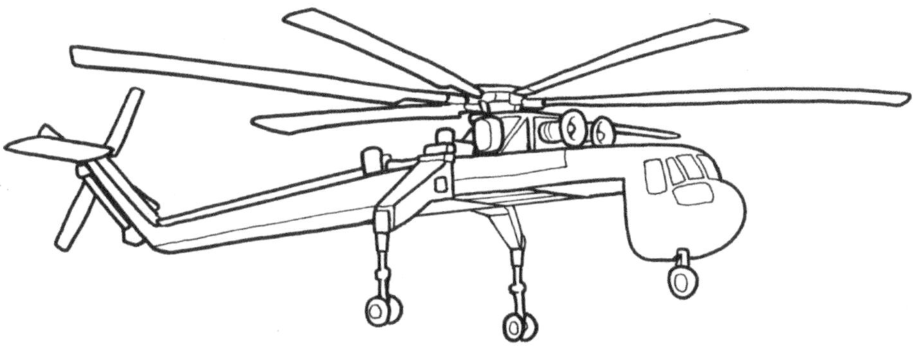

Oops!

Is that how heli-skiing
is supposed to work?

Julio the mechanic is searching for a lost wrench.
Can you help him find it?

The Spaceship Two is gliding through space.

Uh-oh! Chuck broke the nose gear!

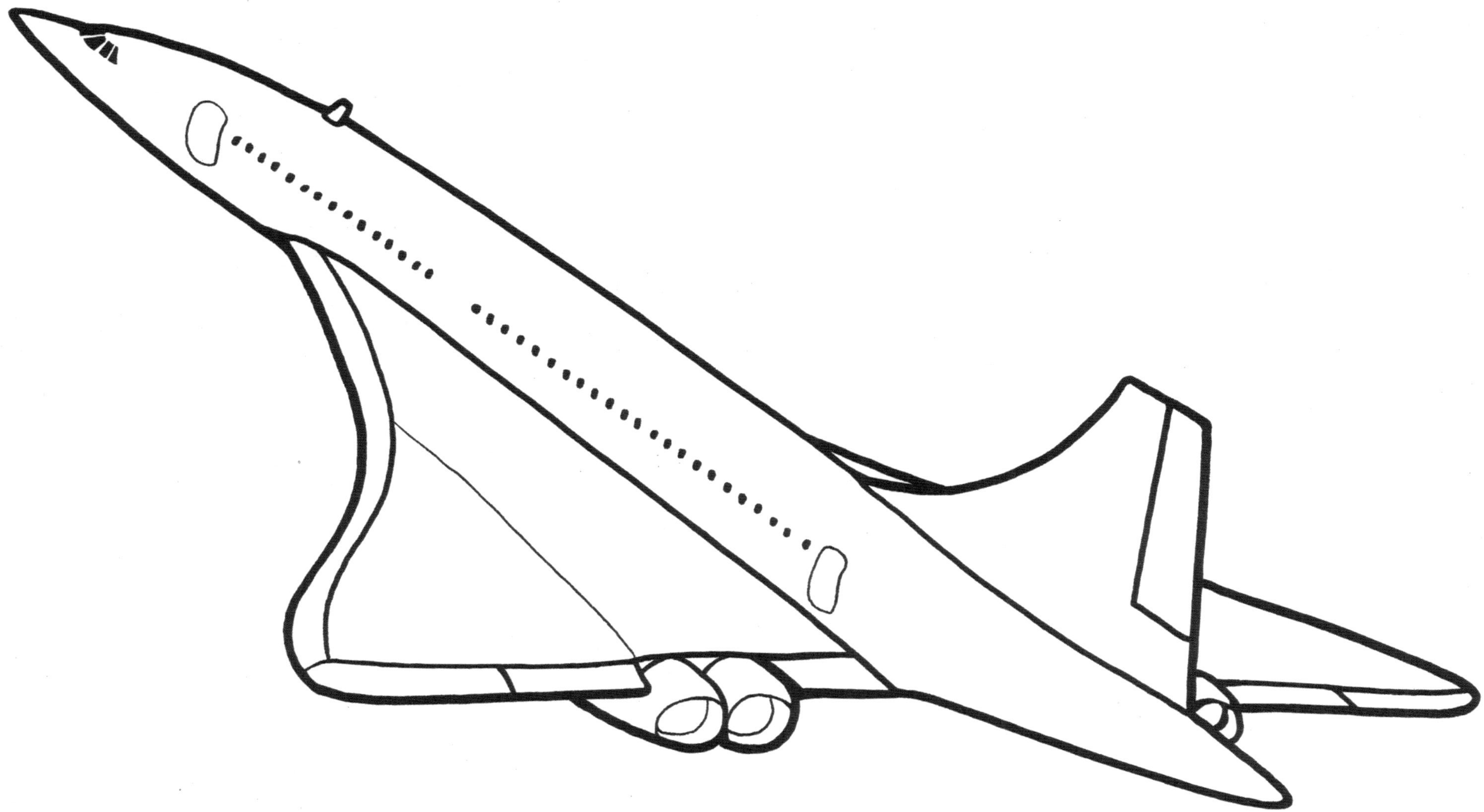

The Aerospatiale-BAC Concorde was the fastest passenger plane in the world.
It flew from 1976 to 2003 and could go as fast as Mach 2.

The Curtiss SB2C-4 Helldiver was a carrier-based dive bomber during World War II.

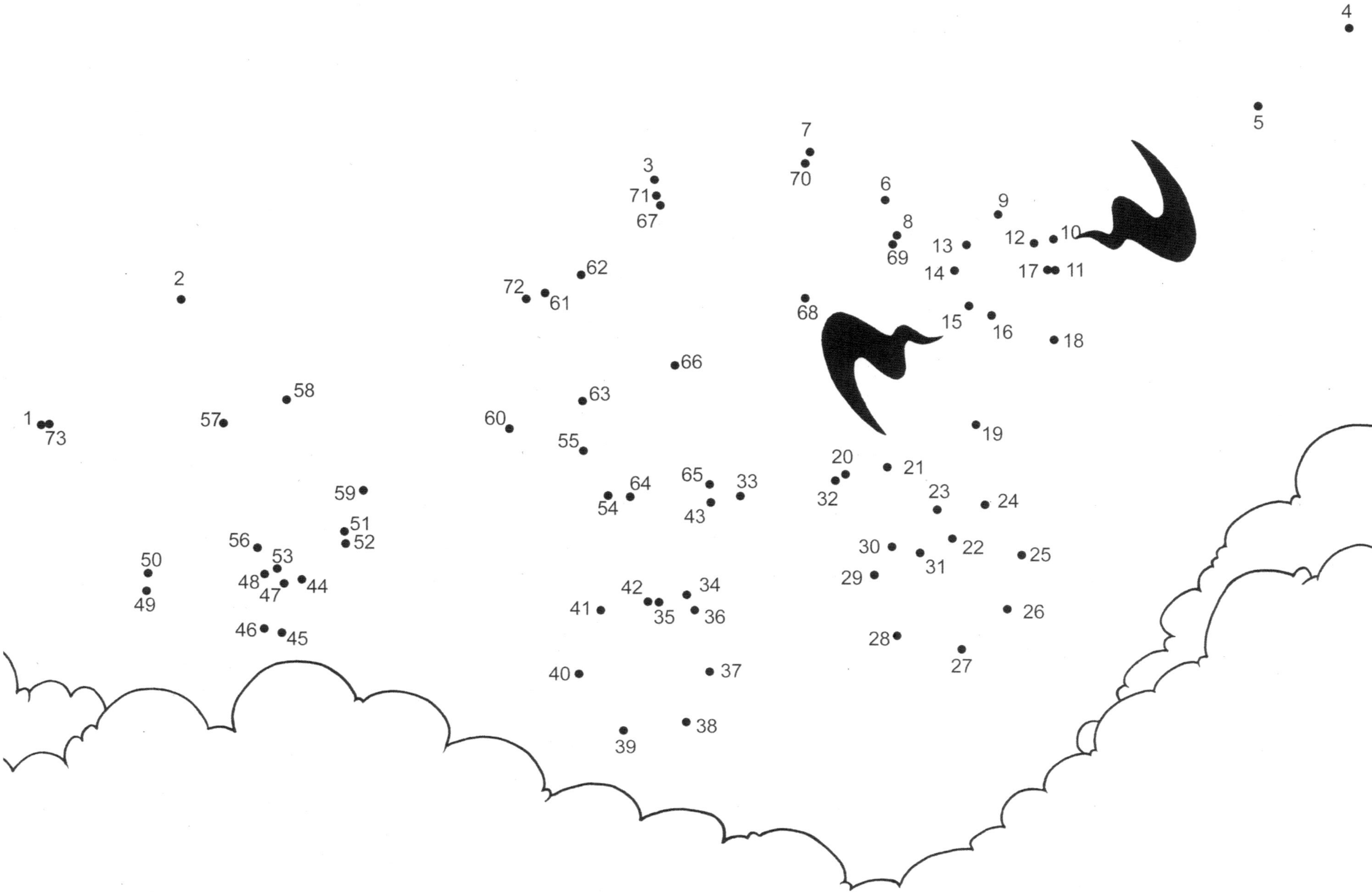

Connect the dots!

The SR-71 Blackbird was able to fly
more than three times the speed of sound.

Solutions

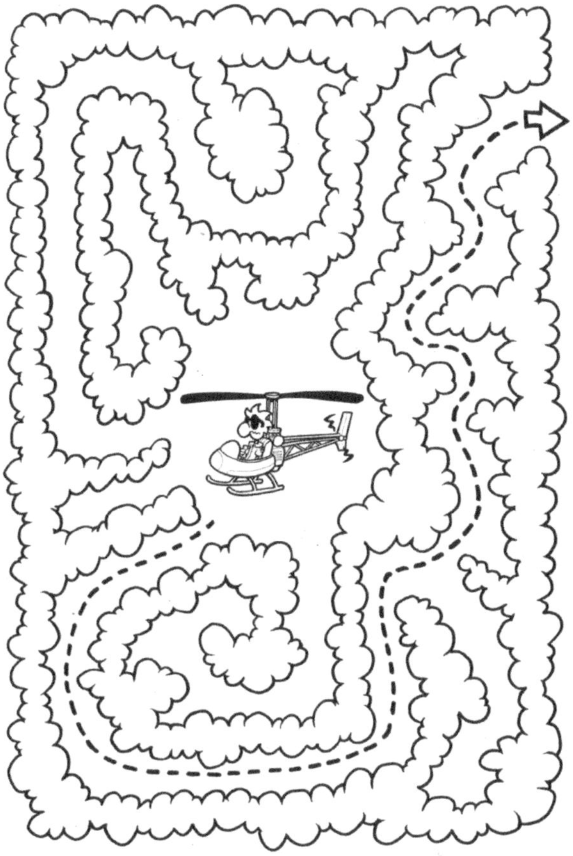

Solution to page 7

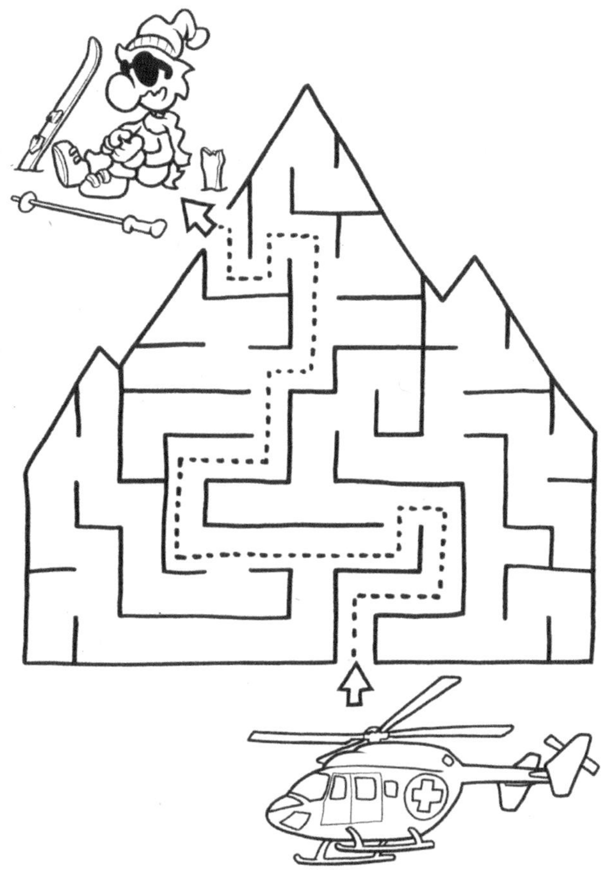

Solution to page 12

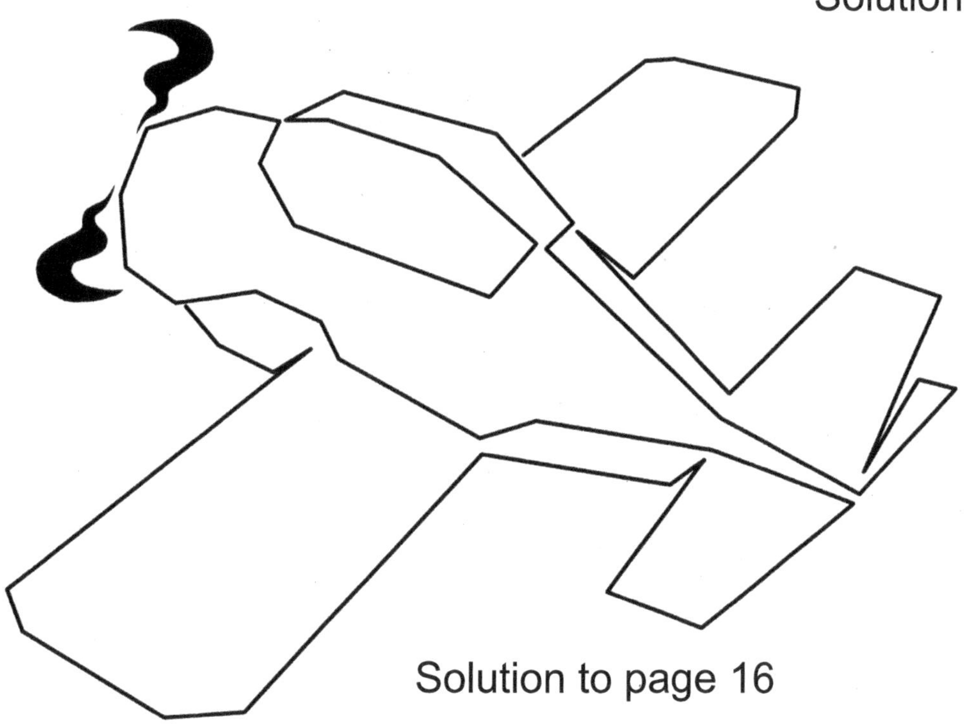

Solution to page 16

Solutions

Can you tell which aircraft transports what cargo?
Draw lines to match the aircraft to the cargo.

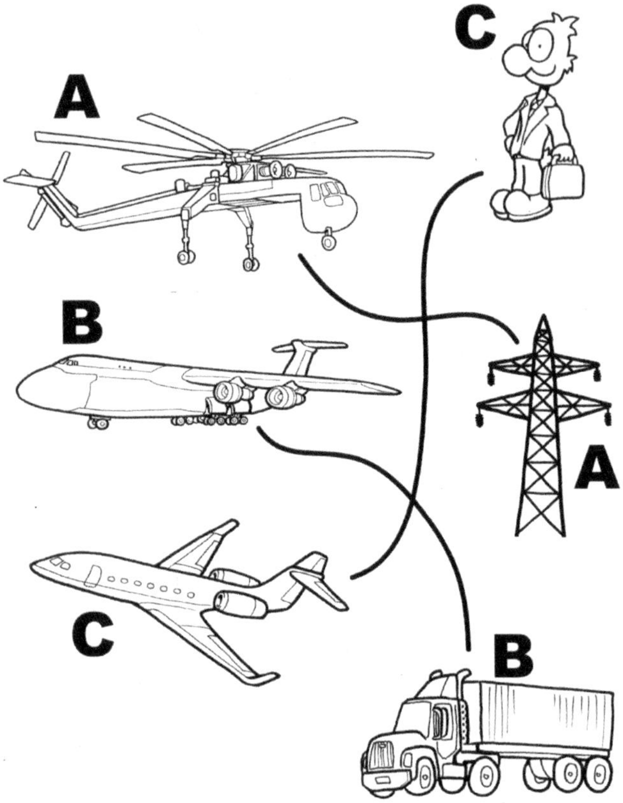

Solution to page 21

Solution to page 24

Solution to page 29

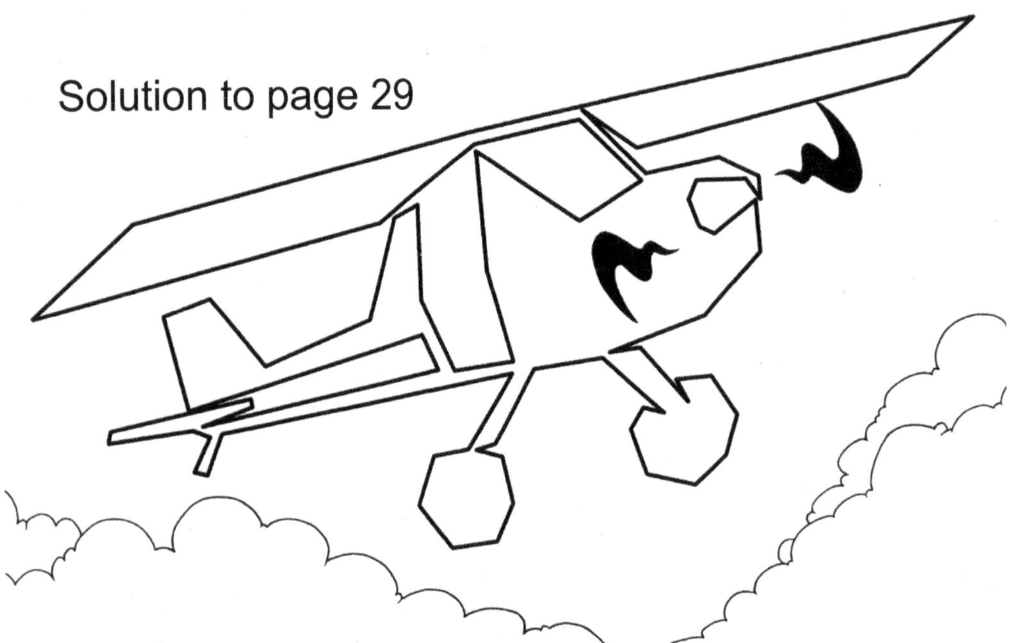